To Benjamin
The hero of the story!

Benjamin Panda and his friends are playing their best-loved game of roly poly.

It is lots of fun and much better than walking.

4

Down and down,

round and round they roll.

Bopping into each other

and bouncing off trees and bushes,

Pandas are so fluffy they never get hurt.

5

Suddenly –

SPLASH!

they roll into an unexpected puddle of water.
Where has it come from? It hasn't been raining!

As they shake the water from their fur,

Benjamin can see that the nearby river has burst its banks and he wonders why.

Benjamin looks downstream and notices that the river is blocked with plastic bottles and other rubbish.
"Oh no!" exclaims Benjamin "the water can't get through."

"We will have to remove the rubbish, or more of the jungle could be flooded. That would be a disaster for our friends and food supply." says Benjamin. But how?

9

Benjamin looks around and sees his friend Tumble is eating some bamboo...

...and this gives him an idea.

10

Benjamin asks Tumble to chomp down two long lengths of bamboo,

while he tears off strips from another piece and cleverly twists the strips into a net.

11

Working together the friends make an amazing makeshift bridge.

They wonder how to get it across the water.

"I know" says the tallest stretchiest monkey, waggling his floppy hands, "I can swing across!"

Using an extra long vine and taking an extra big leap...

12

...the monkey swings safely to the other side, landing like an acrobat.

Bit by bit, Benjamin and his friends push the bamboo bridge across to him. The monkey stretches out his long arms and grabs the bridge, then using some vines he ties the bamboo bridge tightly to a nearby tree.

13

Benjamin carefully shimmies out onto the bridge. Being a bear, he's not scared of climbing.

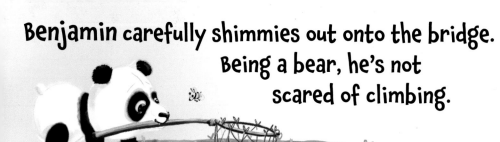

Just as he reaches the middle he loses his grip and starts to slip!

Luckily he manages to hang on with his strong legs and sharp claws. Dangling upside down, he sees that he is close to the rubbish swirling in the water below.

Clinging on to the bridge, Benjamin begins scooping up the nasty rubbish with the net.

15

The other jungle creatures all want to help, so Benjamin passes the rubbish filled net to a monkey...

...who then gives it to the red panda...

...who finally hands it to the tiger!

The tiger empties the rubbish into one big pile.
"Why don't we call ourselves the Eco Crew,
as we are doing such a good job."
says the tiger. "That is a great idea."
says Benjamin.

17

Finally, the last piece of rubbish is collected...

...and the river runs freely again. HOORAY!

18

Tumble the red panda asks where the rubbish came from.

Benjamin explains that instead of recycling it,

some people just throw their rubbish on the ground and a lot of it ends up in rivers and even in the SEA!

"That is terrible," says the red panda.
"We should remind everyone that –
If everybody does their bit
the planet will be fighting fit."

Benjamin and the Eco Crew stand in front of the big pile of rubbish, happy with doing their bit to help.

The end